THIS BOOK BELONGS TO:

....

ART SPARKS

IGNITE YOUR IMAGINATION WITH CREATIVE PROMPTS INSPIRED BY REAL MASTERPIECES

WRITTEN BY: ALICE HARMAN

ILLUSTRATED BY: KIMBERLIE CLINTHORNE-WONG

YOU WILL NEED

On these pages you'll find the ESSENTIAL ART MATERIALS you will need for the activities in this book. You will also need:

- Paper
- Aluminum foil
- Cardboard scraps
- Paper scraps
- Fabric scraps
- Mark-making tools, such as a toothpick, comb, chopsticks, or a spoon
- Bar of soap (ideally a softer, creamier type)
- Modeling clay

STRING

MARKERS

COLORED PENCILS

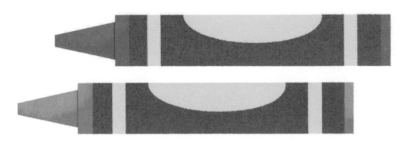

CRAYONS

These materials are OPTIONAL:
- Food coloring
- Plain ceramic tile(s)
- Craft glue
- Large piece of fabric
- Newspapers and magazines to cut up
- Cardboard box
- Styrofoam container or craft foam
- T-shirt
- Fabric paint

GLUE STICK

PAPER CLIPS

PENCIL

ERASER

SAFETY SCISSORS

ACRYLIC PAINT

PAINT BRUSHES

HOW TO USE THIS BOOK

Welcome to The Metropolitan Museum of Art! If you like, you can call it The Met for short.

In this book, you'll discover some fascinating artworks from all over the world and have the chance to try out all sorts of arty ideas and techniques to create your own masterpieces.

There are more than 20 paintings, sculptures, drawings, and other works of art for you to learn about. Each one has a related creative activity so you can have a go too!

But that's not all. You'll also find fun mini-activities dotted throughout the book. These are designed to spark your imagination and help you look at things a bit differently, just like a great artist does.

Some of the activities inside are more difficult than others, so ask your adult if you need help, especially when using equipment that can cause injury, such as scissors.

So, are you ready?

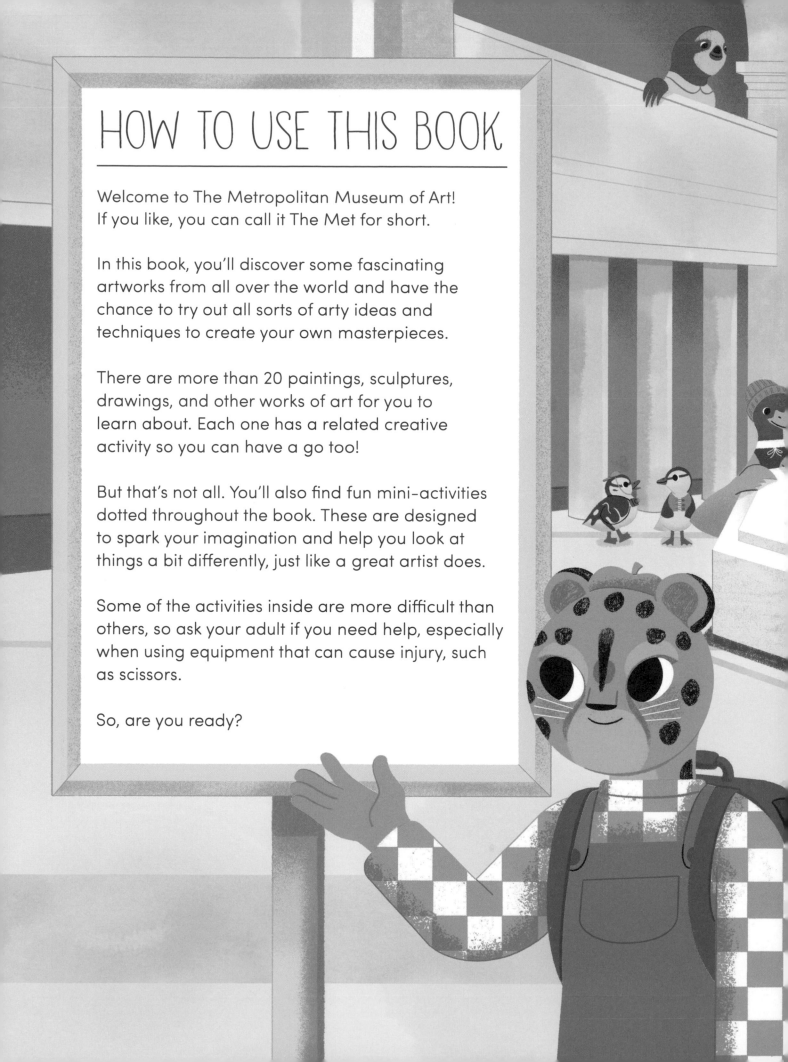

LET'S START
CREATING!

LET'S DRAW PEOPLE!

Bill Traylor was an African American artist who spent his life creating more than 1,000 drawings and paintings. Traylor drew people he saw around town, showing their character through their poses and the objects that they held. He often used sharp lines, solid colors, and bold patterns in his art.

Bill Traylor
Two Men Walking
c. 1939–43

TRY TO TELL A STORY THROUGH YOUR DRAWINGS. WHAT IS HAPPENING? HOW DO THESE PEOPLE FEEL ABOUT EACH OTHER?

Can you complete these line drawings to create your own characters? Try giving each one a colorful outfit and some accessories. Show off their personalities!

Fill this space with bold paintings and drawings of people you see out and about. Try using a mixture of crayons, marker pens, paint, and colored pencils.

Think about the people's body language. How might they sit or stand? What hand gestures might they make? What objects could they hold that might tell us something about them.

Noticed any similarities in how you draw your characters? This is your own

ARTISTIC STYLE!

TRAYLOR CREATED MORE THAN 1,000 DRAWINGS AND PAINTINGS ON SCRAP CARDBOARD! USE CARDBOARD SCRAPS TO CREATE YOUR NEXT MASTERPIECE.

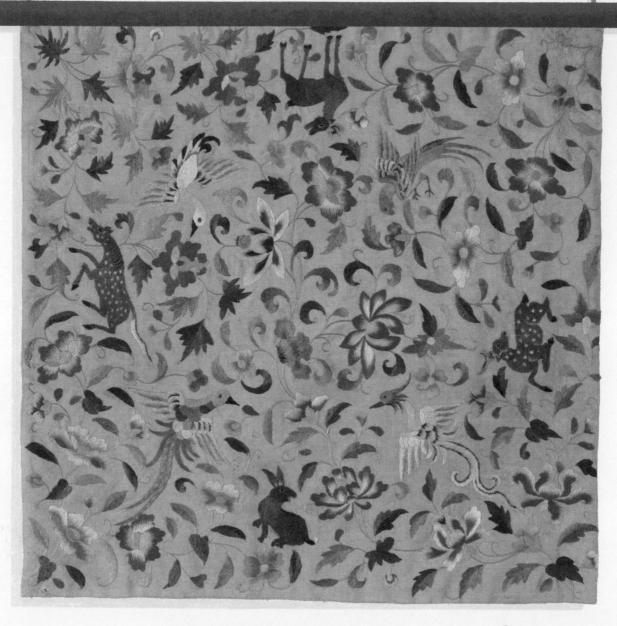

Textile with Animals, Birds, and Flowers
Eastern Central Asia, late 12th–14th century

MAKING MOTIFS

This textile has nature-inspired motifs sewn all over it
in silk thread. A motif is like an ingredient in an artwork.
It can appear once or many times. Which leaf, flower,
and animal motifs repeat in the artwork above?
Which of them appear only once?

Choose your three favorite nature-inspired motifs from the previous page.
Fill the space below by drawing them yourself, over and over again.
How could you make these motifs connect up or fit around each other?

NOT INTO NATURE?
BASE YOUR MOTIFS ON
ANYTHING YOU LIKE—SPORTS,
MAGIC, VIDEO GAMES, OR
JUST RANDOM SHAPES.

MAKE YOUR OWN HERALDIC SYMBOL

Can you see what the little gold decorations on this armor are? They're quite tricky to make out, but maybe you've spotted that they are all castles, lions, or curved shapes that look a bit like flowers.

These are heraldic symbols—pictures designed to represent certain people, families, armies, or other groups. This armor was made for a five-year-old prince, and the symbols represent his three royal family lines: Castile (castle), León (lion), and France (fleur-de-lis).

Armor of Infante Luis, Prince of Asturias
Signature probably refers to Jean Drouart
1712

Quickly sketch anything that reminds you of the different members of your family or friend group. It could be something they like, an activity you do together, a favorite memory, a silly joke you share, or anything else! Aim to draw between five and ten different things.

TRY ADDING
SHAPES AND COLORS
THAT REMIND YOU OF
PEOPLE AS WELL AS
REALISTIC OBJECTS.

Circle the three drawings on the previous page that stand out most to you. Combine different parts of these drawings to create your own heraldic symbol for your family or friend group. It can be as silly or strange as you like!

Draw your heraldic symbol design onto the T-shirt on the opposite page. Imagine your friends or family all wearing it together!

If you like, maybe you could even ask your adult to help you decorate real T-shirts with your heraldic symbol. You will need special fabric paint for this. You can use the shape to the left or the one below as a template.

WANT SOMETHING A BIT MORE DRAMATIC? TRY DESIGNING A SUIT OF ARMOR OR A SUPERHERO COSTUME THAT FEATURES YOUR HERALDIC SYMBOL!

PAINTING BY DOTS

Georges Seurat
Circus Sideshow
1887–88

Look closely at this painting.
What do you see?

≥ DOTS! ≤

Thousands of tiny
colored dots.

Can you use the prompts below to create an image
using only dots of color? You could use paints,
markers, or colored pencils.

A cat

An apple

Your face

MIX THINGS UP BY USING
GIANT DOTS OR DOTS OF
ALL DIFFERENT SIZES.

Georges Seurat's painting uses dark, shadowy colors to show an evening scene. Imagine it in daytime, painted in light, bright colors. How would it feel different? Try painting two versions of the same scene in the boxes below with different colored dots to give a feel of different times of day.

Use light, bright colors here...

... and dark, shadowy colors here.

TURN YOUR PAINTBRUSH AROUND AND USE THE HARD END TO MAKE DOTS.

Clara Peeters
A Bouquet of Flowers
c. 1612

CREATE A STILL LIFE

A still life is an artwork showing an arrangement of objects that do not move—often cut flowers, fruit, or household items such as bowls or glasses.

Clara Peeters painted flowers in incredibly realistic detail. Her fine brushstrokes captured everything from the delicate curl of a petal to a drop of dew on a leaf.

Can you see how Peeters uses different shades to add detail and depth to her flowers? Where did she use lighter colors? Where did she use darker ones? Try coloring in this rose to match Peeters's painting.

PEETERS'S STILL LIFES OFTEN HAVE HEAVY BLACK BACKGROUNDS. TRY COLORING AROUND YOUR ROSE WITH BLACK PAINT OR PEN. HOW DOES IT CHANGE HOW THE FLOWER LOOKS?

Paul Cézanne
Still Life with Apples and Pears
1891–92

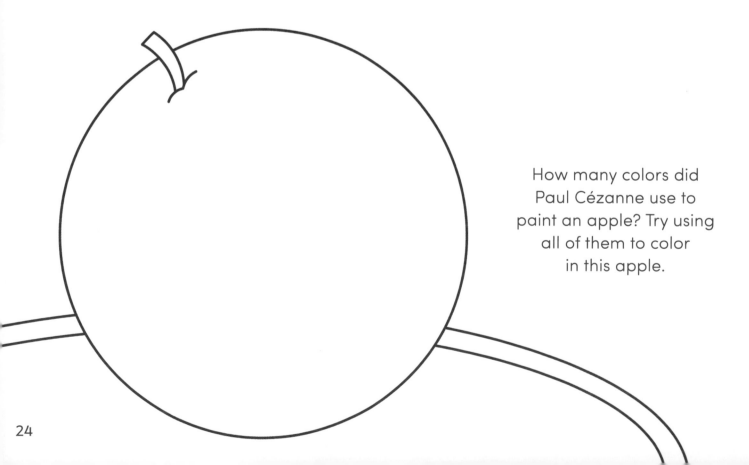

How many colors did
Paul Cézanne use to
paint an apple? Try using
all of them to color
in this apple.

Juan Gris
The Musician's Table
1914

Can you fill in this violin by sticking down overlapping scraps of paper to create an effect like Juan Gris's artwork?

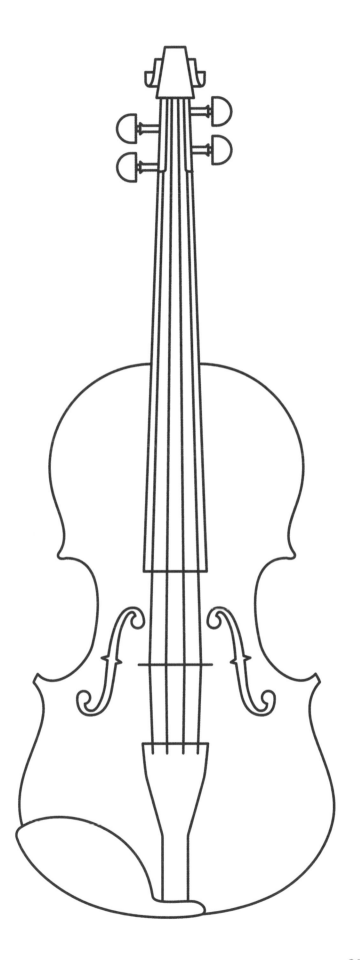

SMART SYMMETRY

This sculpture uses symmetry. Do you recognize that word? It means when parts of a shape—or an artwork in this case— balance or match each other, often across its center.

Can you see the ways the figures are symmetrical (the same) and asymmetrical (different)? The symmetry of the two people in this sculpture shows the balance and connection between them.

Let's try and create a symmetrical artwork...

Figure: Seated Couple
Dogon artist
18th–early 19th century

1 Fold a piece of A4 paper in half. Draw an outline of a person on it, making sure that one of their arms reaches the folded edge.

FOLD OR SCRUNCH THE LEFTOVER PAPER SCRAPS TO MAKE DIFFERENT FEATURES AND ACCESSORIES TO STICK ON EACH PAPER PERSON.

2 Pinch the two sides of the paper together and cut around the outline. This way, you'll cut through both sides at once. Do not cut around the end of the arm at the fold.

3 Open out your symmetrical pair of people holding hands!

CREATIVE CALLIGRAPHY

Abd al-Qadir Hisari
Calligraphic Galleon
dated 1180 AH/1766–67 CE

Calligraphy is the art of writing beautifully with a pen or brush.
Calligraphic artworks sometimes combine this writing with drawn
or painted images, like the one above. Can you see the calligraphy
on the boat and in the lines that make up the waves and border?
Experiment with the style of your calligraphy. Try tracing over the
letter "A" below. Which style do you like best?

Aa   Aa   Aa

Calligraphy often features elaborate flicks and strokes. Can you use calligraphy to write your name? Try adding one or more of the flourishes below to the letters. You can use a pen or paint and a thin brush—or combine the two!

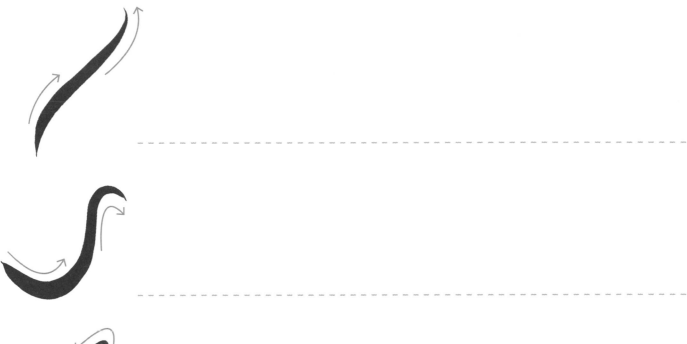

DECORATE YOUR NAME BY DRAWING OR PAINTING TINY LINES, CIRCLES, OR OTHER PATTERNS AROUND THE LETTERS.

Fill these drawings with beautiful, colorful writing that tell us about them. You can write a fun description, a story, or even a poem!

MAKE AN ANIMAL PENDANT

This is a pendant: a piece of jewelry that you can wear around your neck on a string or chain. This one looks like a tree frog that lives in the forests of Costa Rica, which is where experts believe it was made.

This pendant is made from solid gold, but you can make your own version using cardboard and aluminum foil!

Frog Pendant
Chiriquí
11th–16th century

Draw the simple outline of an animal in this box. Try to keep the details big and bold, like the artist who made the frog pendant did.

You can get creative with changing or exaggerating some of your animal's features—like the frog's curly two-forked tongue or its supersize feet!

2 Copy your design onto a piece of cardboard or cardstock and cut it out.

3 Wrap the cardboard or cardstock in aluminum foil, pressing down tightly.

4

Ask your adult to punch a hole in the top of your pendant and put it on a string to wear!

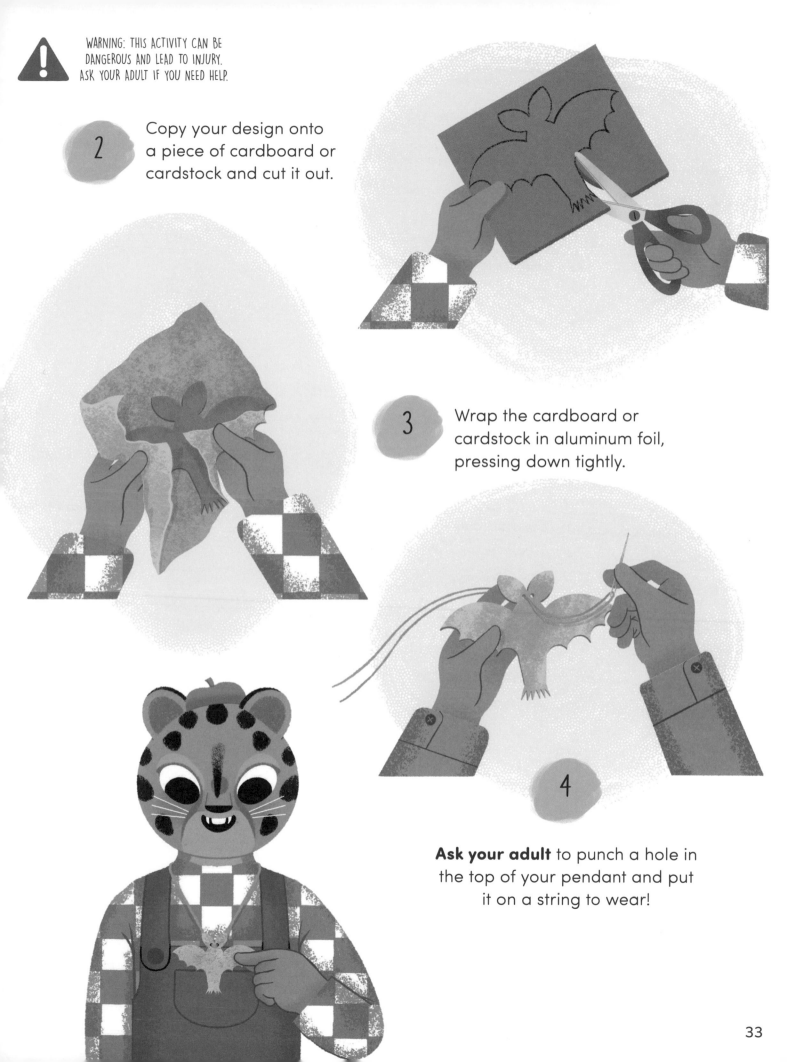

33

PAINT A SURREAL SELF-PORTRAIT

Leonora Carrington
Self-Portrait
c. 1937–38

This painting looks like some sort of strange dream, doesn't it? The oddly empty room, the rocking horse floating up on the wall, and a hyena?! Leonora Carrington was a surrealist artist. Her art explores dreams, hidden thoughts, and the unusual or unexpected.

A self-portrait is a work of art that you create about yourself. Carrington has painted herself here with objects that give us a peek inside her mind.

Try quickly sketching a few objects that say something about you... your favorite toy, a wild animal that reminds you of yourself, a food you really like, a magical creature, or your favorite item of clothing.
Don't think too much—just draw!

KEEP A NOTEBOOK BY YOUR BED. AS SOON AS YOU WAKE UP, DRAW WHATEVER YOU REMEMBER FROM YOUR DREAMS.

In this room, draw yourself and the objects you just sketched on the previous page. But try mixing them up in impossible, dreamlike ways. Maybe a unicorn is wearing your best sneakers, or a dolphin is eating your pizza!

Decorate the room, too. You could do this in the same colors as your home. Dreams can sometimes feel strangest when familiar things combine with bizarre and impossible ones.

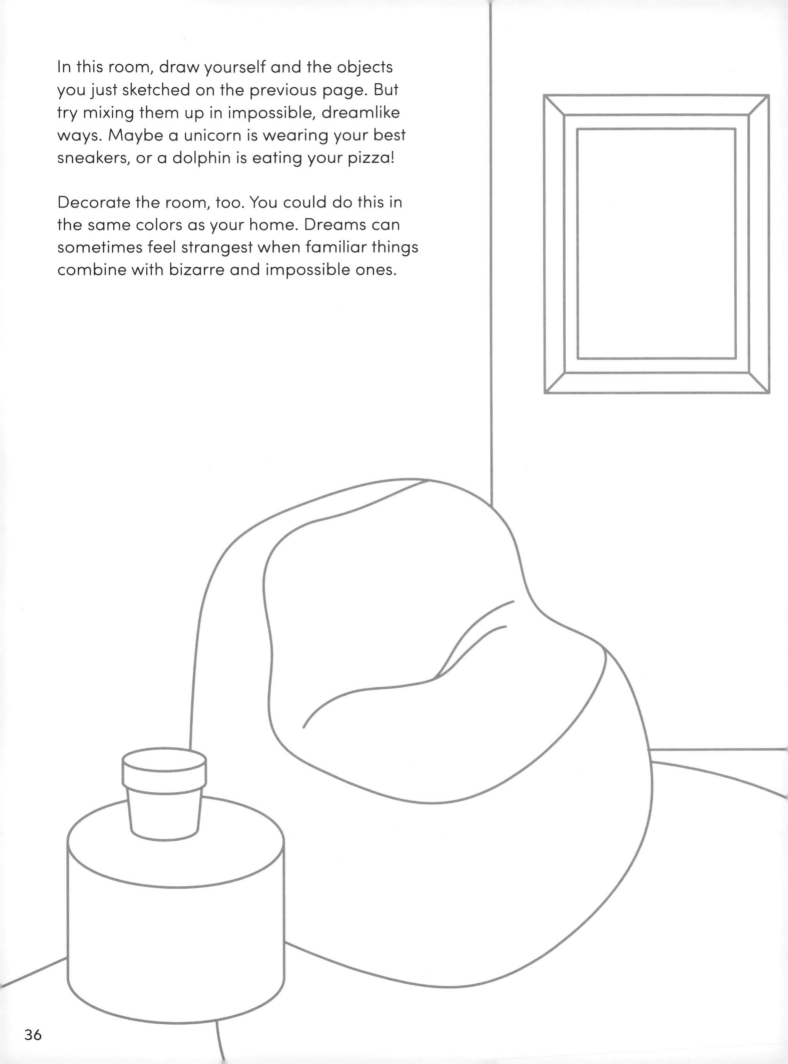

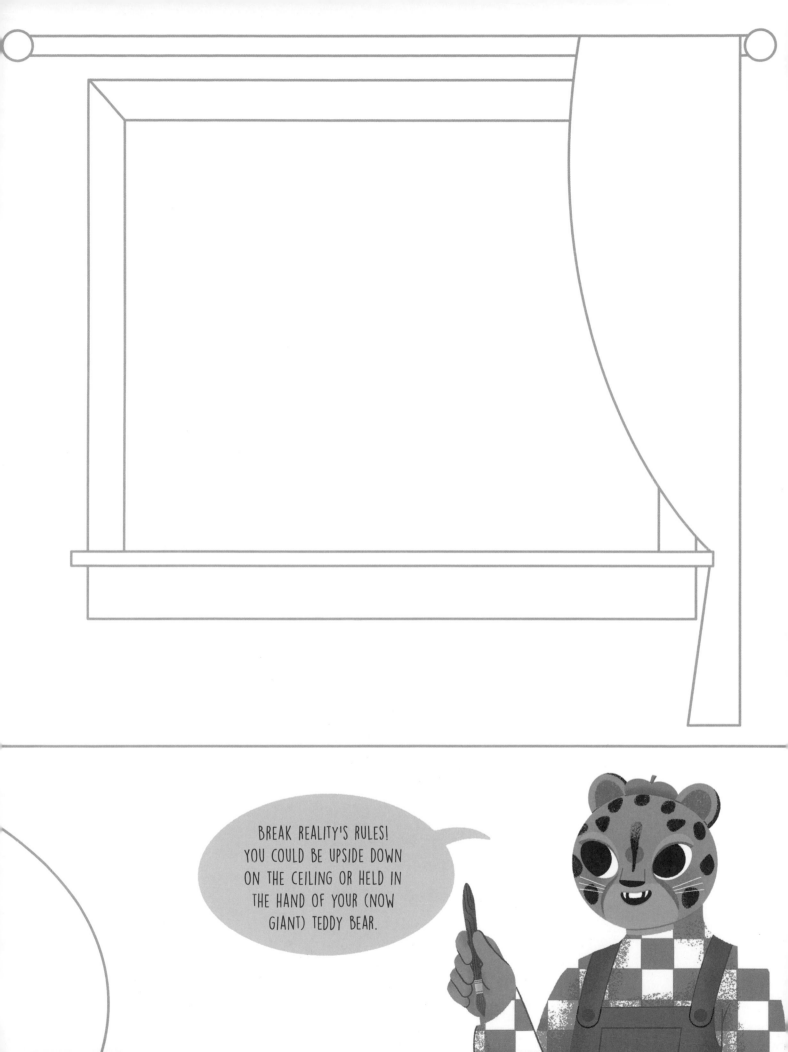

LET'S DECORATE WITH MARK-MAKING!

This ancient Greek flask is made out of terracotta (a reddish-brown clay). The black decorative figures were painted on in slip (a more liquid form of clay) that turns black when heated.

This type of decoration can be tricky, so let's try a different way to get the same effect. Instead of drawing onto a surface, we can decorate by scratching color away.

Terracotta lekythos (oil flask)
Attributed to the Amasis Painter
c. 550–530 BCE

Ask your adult to help you find three objects around the home that are safe to use. You could use a coin, an old comb, a craft stick, a spoon, or chopsticks.

Use colored pencils or markers to fill in these circles. Then use a black crayon to cover over all the color. Once all the color is covered, use a different object in each circle to scratch off the black crayon in a pattern to reveal the color underneath. How do different tools make the marks look?

ASK YOUR ADULT TO HELP YOU COLLECT OBJECTS FROM NATURE FOR THIS MARK—MAKING. YOU COULD TRY TWIGS, BARK, OR STONES.

Let's use what we learned on the last page and color in this vase shape with orange or red colored pencils or markers. Then go over it with black crayon.

You can decorate the vase with all sorts of lines, shapes, and patterns. You could try straight lines, dots, zigzags, curved lines, or anything you like!

Color in this vase shape the same way—first using colored pencils or markers and then black crayon over the top. This time, you could try decorating the vase with people.

First, scratch their outlines into the black crayon. Leaving these figures black, scratch away all the crayon around them to reveal the orange or red background.

Keep your outlines simple at first, and use the scratching tool that's easiest to handle!

USE DIFFERENT COLORS UNDERNEATH THE BLACK CRAYON LAYER SO THAT WHEN YOU SCRATCH, IT REVEALS A RAINBOW WORLD.

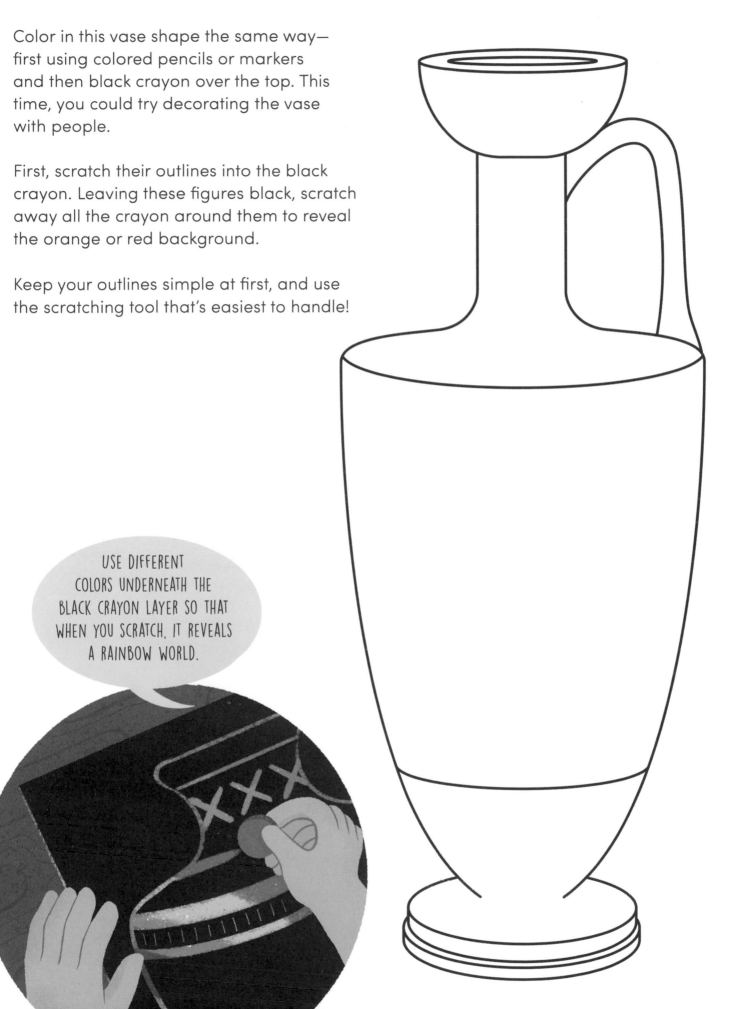

WEAVE A TAPESTRY

This tapestry was made to be hung up inside a home. Its creator used just a few colors and shapes to develop a complex design.

Look closely at all the different ways these patterns use rectangles, straight lines, and triangles.

HOW MANY DIFFERENT PATTERNS CAN YOU SPOT?

Temne peoples
Interior hanging, 19th century

Create your own tapestry design by filling in this grid with different shapes.
Use circles, hexagons, stars, or any other shape you can think of. You could even
invent a new shape! Try coloring it in with just two or three different colors.

The tapestry on page 42 is made up of thousands of colored threads joined together using a technique called weaving. Let's try weaving a paper tapestry!

1

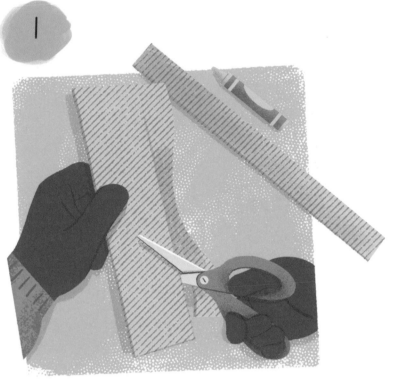

Use a ruler to draw a 5in x 5in square on a piece of paper. Divide this square into five 1in-wide strips. Color half of the strips in a pale color, and half in a dark color. Then, cut out the strips.

2

Lay the pale strings vertically in the space marked on the next page. Stick all of them down at both ends using sticky tape.

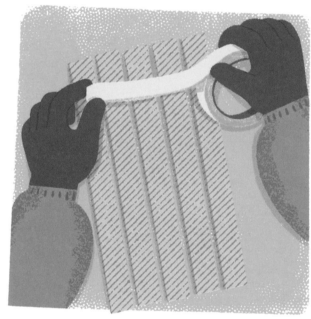

3

Starting at the top left, weave a dark strip over and then under the pale strips until you run out. Stick down both ends of the dark strip using sticky tape. Below the first dark strip, repeat the last step, but go under and then over the pale strips. Continue until you've woven in all the dark strips.

STICK YOUR PAPER STRIPS HERE!

- -

CREATE A FEW PAPER
TAPESTRIES, THEN STICK THEM
ONTO A SHEET OF CARDBOARD.
ADD LINES, TRIANGLE PATTERNS,
AND AREAS OF SOLID COLOR,
AS IN THE TEMNE TAPESTRY.

LET'S MAKE TILE ART!

Garden Gathering
1640–50

This glamorous garden party has been painted across a tiled wall.
The tiles join together to create one big picture. Pick one of the tiles
from the painting. Can you recreate it in the tile below?

Can you draw and color in your own dream party below?
Try using the same six colors for the whole picture. Then,
why not try recreating your party picture on ceramic tiles?

LET YOUR IMAGINATION
RUN FREE! WOULD YOUR DREAM
PARTY HAVE ROBOT WAITERS?
WILD ANIMAL GUESTS? A CAKE
AS BIG AS A TREE?!

DESIGN UNIQUE CERAMICS

George Ohr didn't want his ceramics—including mugs, vases, and teapots—to look too perfect. He squished, poked, and twisted his creations into unique, unexpected shapes to make them more interesting.

Try closing your eyes and using the hand you don't usually write with or your feet to draw a cup on the next page. Add color and decoration. Aim for interesting, not perfect!

George E. Ohr
Teapot
c. 1897–1900

WHY NOT MAKE YOUR CUP OUT OF MUD! USE STICKS TO SCRATCH IN PATTERNS AND ADD LEAVES AND OTHER NATURAL OBJECTS FOR DECORATION.

Ohr dug and prepared his own clay, which is a lot of work! Try making the cup you've drawn out of modeling clay instead.

CREATE AN ANIMAL RELIEF

Panel with striding lion
Babylonian
c. 604–562 BCE

Take a good look at this magnificent lion. It's painted on a brick wall, but it doesn't look flat, does it? That's because this lion is a relief. It has 3-D parts, made of clay, that stand out from the brick wall. Want to try making a lion relief? Follow these steps!

⚠ WARNING: THIS ACTIVITY CAN BE DANGEROUS AND LEAD TO INJURY. ASK YOUR ADULT IF YOU NEED HELP.

1. Trace the shapes on the next page onto a piece of paper.

2. Cut out the paper shapes and trace around them onto a piece of cardboard.

3. Cut out the cardboard shapes, and stick them together in the order shown on the next page.

4. Paint on color and details such as eyes, a mouth, and whiskers to bring your lion to life.

ROOOAAARRR!

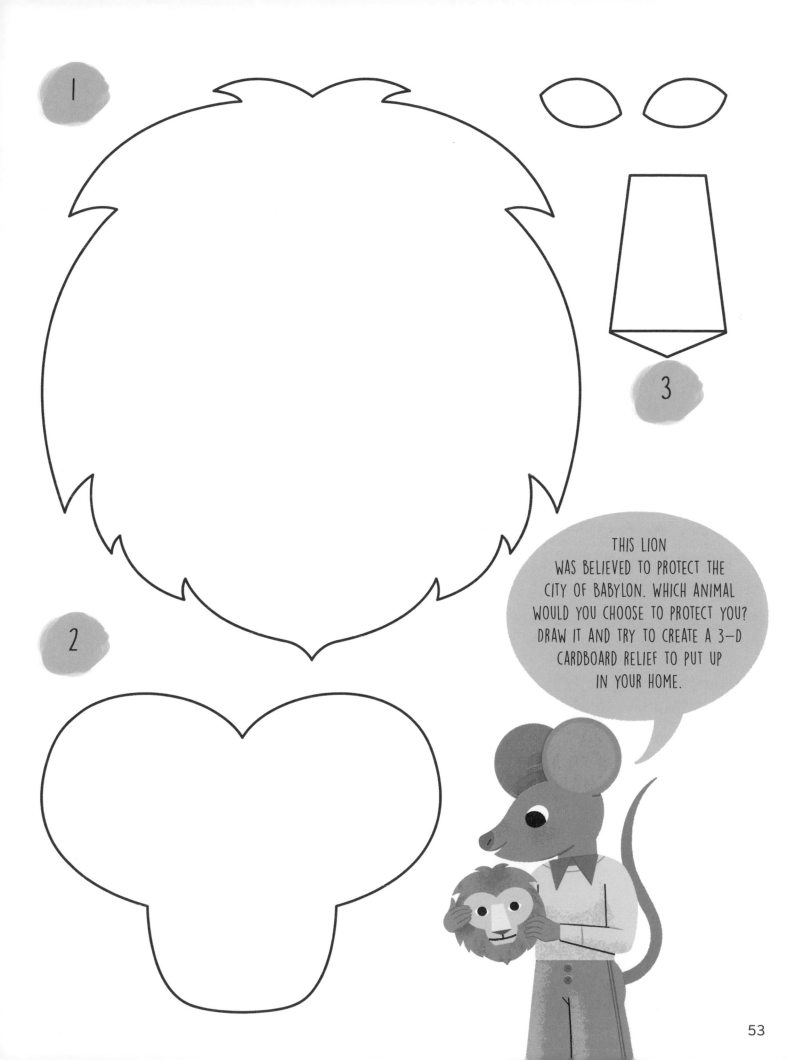

1

2

3

THIS LION
WAS BELIEVED TO PROTECT THE
CITY OF BABYLON. WHICH ANIMAL
WOULD YOU CHOOSE TO PROTECT YOU?
DRAW IT AND TRY TO CREATE A 3-D
CARDBOARD RELIEF TO PUT UP
IN YOUR HOME.

CREATE A COLLAGE

Faith Ringgold
Street Story Quilt
1985

This is one of Faith Ringgold's "story quilts." It shows an apartment building at three different moments across 30 years. Ringgold uses pictures and words to tell the stories of the people who live here.

Sewing a quilt can be tricky, so let's try another way to get this patchwork effect. We'll use collage: a way of making art by sticking pieces of different materials—often paper and fabric—onto a surface.

Decorate the house on the next page by sticking on paper or fabric scraps. What's going on in the house? Add in people and objects to tell a story and writing, too, if you like.

TRY ADDING PICTURES, WORDS, AND PATTERNS CUT OUT FROM OLD NEWSPAPERS, MAGAZINES, OR JUNK MAIL ONTO YOUR COLLAGE. ASK YOUR ADULT BEFORE YOU CUT ANYTHING!

Use what you've learned to create your own collage comic book! First, what's your main character's name?

_____

Now, let's make up a four-part story:

1. Your main character has a BIG PROBLEM. What is it?

_____

_____

2. How do they try to SOLVE THEIR PROBLEM?

_____

_____

3. What GETS IN THEIR WAY and makes things HARDER?

_____

_____

4. What happens IN THE END?

_____

_____

_____

Draw your story into these squares, and write it in the space underneath. Use one square for each part of your story. Stick down paper and fabric scraps to fill your drawings with color and pattern.

MAKE A MODEL BOAT

Model Sporting Boat
Ancient Egypt
c. 1981–1975 BCE

This amazingly detailed wooden model boat shows ancient Egyptians on a hunting and fishing trip. Rich people liked to take these boat trips on the Nile river. They watched as the hunters and fishers speared fish with long spikes and caught water birds to eat.

Try making your own model boat! Cut out the shapes on the next page and trace around them onto cardboard or cardstock. Cut out as many people, waves, and pairs of oars as you want. Decorate all of your cardboard pieces and then stick them together as shown.

FIND A BIT OF WOOD OR TREE BARK TO USE FOR YOUR BOAT'S BASE!

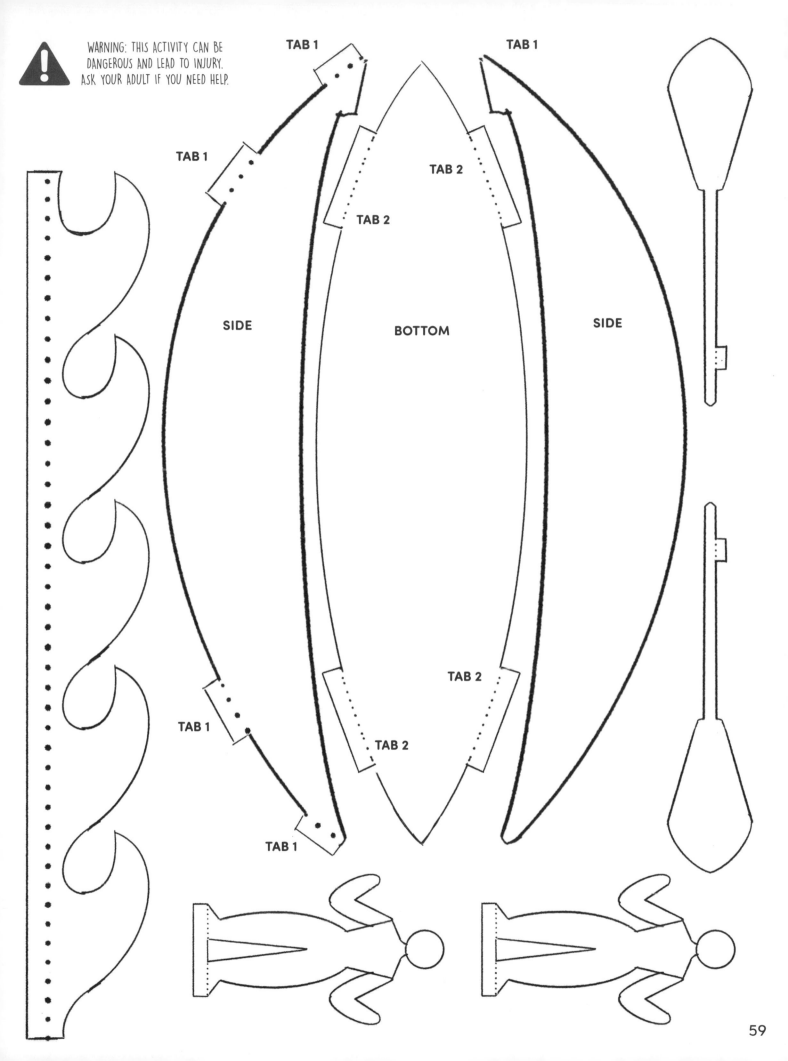

WARNING: THIS ACTIVITY CAN BE DANGEROUS AND LEAD TO INJURY. ASK YOUR ADULT IF YOU NEED HELP.

TAB 1

TAB 1

TAB 1

TAB 2

TAB 2

SIDE

BOTTOM

SIDE

TAB 2

TAB 2

TAB 1

TAB 1

COLOR ME IN!

1 Use the dotted line as a guide and fold all Tab 1's upward and all Tab 2's downward. Slot the bottom and the sides of the boat together and use the tabs to make it sturdy.

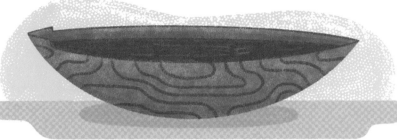

2 Use the dotted line as a guide and fold along the bottom of the people. Push the excess cardboard under so that it is hidden behind their feet. Place the people into the boat standing up.

3 Use the tab at the oar's end to rest it in the person's arm. Fold over the person's arm so that it is gripping the top of the oar. Rest the other end of the oar on the surface of the boat.

4 Use the dotted line as a guide and fold along the bottom of the waves. Push the excess cardboard under so that it is hidden behind the waves. Then, stand the waves up on a surface around the boat.

Katsushika Hokusai
Under the Wave off Kanagawa (Kanagawa
oki nami ura), also known as The Great Wave
c. 1830–32

LET'S MAKE WOODBLOCK-STYLE PRINTS!

Katsushika Hokusai carved complex, nature-inspired designs into blocks of wood. He then covered them in colored ink and pressed them onto paper. This technique is known as *ukiyo-e* (woodblock printing).

Many artists made Japan's Mount Fuji the huge, majestic center of attention. But not Hokusai! Can you see how he has played with perspective (see pages 70–73) in the artwork above to show a HUGE wave about to crash over the tiny mountain?

Try drawing something from nature yourself—maybe a leaf,
flower, or insect. Experiment to create different looks.

Try drawing a natural object
in three lines or fewer. First
with a pen or pencil...

... and then with paint and a brush.

Next, try drawing it without lifting your
pen or pencil from the paper at all...

... and then repeat this
with your paint and brush.

How does each drawing feel different?
How does it change the look?

You can use an old Styrofoam container (make sure it's clean) or crafting foam to make a carved woodblock-style print.

1 First, cut out the bottom part of the Styrofoam container.

2 Draw a nature-inspired design onto it with a pen or pencil. You could use one of the techniques you tried on page 63. Press quite hard—but not so hard you tear the foam!

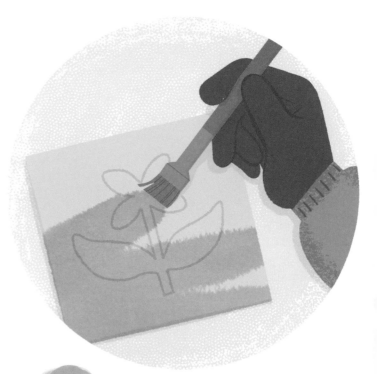

3 Either paint around the design or cover the whole foam piece so that the paint goes into the lines you've carved. The different techniques will give your finished piece slightly different looks.

ADD PEOPLE INTO YOUR WOODBLOCK PRINTS. MAKE THEM TINY TO SHOW NATURE'S GREAT POWER!

Carefully press a sheet of paper onto the foam sheet.
Then, slowly peel it off to reveal your printed design!

PRINT IT HERE

MAKING MOSAICS

A mosaic is a picture or pattern made by covering a surface with
lots of tiny stuck-down pieces of stone, glass, or other hard materials.
Can you see how lines and shapes of different-colored tiles create
the peacock's glorious feathers and the buds of the flowers?

Choose an animal, then quickly draw it in the
blank space at the top of the opposite page.

Mosaic with a Peacock and Flowers
Roman or Byzantine
3rd–4th century

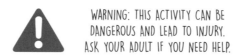

These small squares will be your mosaic tiles. Fill each row with a color from your animal drawing. Remember colors for smaller features, such as eyes and mouth, too. You might want to leave a few squares blank so that you can make extra tiles if you need to.

Then, cut out your colored tiles.

COLOR ME IN!

Draw the outline of your animal below, filling as much of the space as possible. Try organizing your mosaic tiles into piles of different colors to make things easier. Then, stick down the right color squares in the right places to create your mosaic animal.

MIX UP LINES AND PATCHES OF LIGHTER AND DARKER TILES TO GIVE YOUR MOSAIC ARTWORK MORE TEXTURE AND DETAIL. LOOK BACK AT THE PEACOCK MOSAIC FOR INSPIRATION.

Claude Monet
Bridge over a Pond of Water Lilies
1899

PAINTING WITH PERSPECTIVE

Can you see the water lily plants floating on the water? As you move your
eyes up the painting, do they look closer or farther away? Farther away, right?
But this is just paint on a flat canvas! So how did Claude Monet create
this 3-D illusion of depth? He used something called perspective.

This is a way of using lines, color, and sizing to mimic how our eyes see.
It's quite tricky to understand, so let's see it in action...

Cut out these two identical pictures of a frog on a lily pad. Stick one at the bottom of the pond picture, and the other toward the top of the stream. What do you notice?

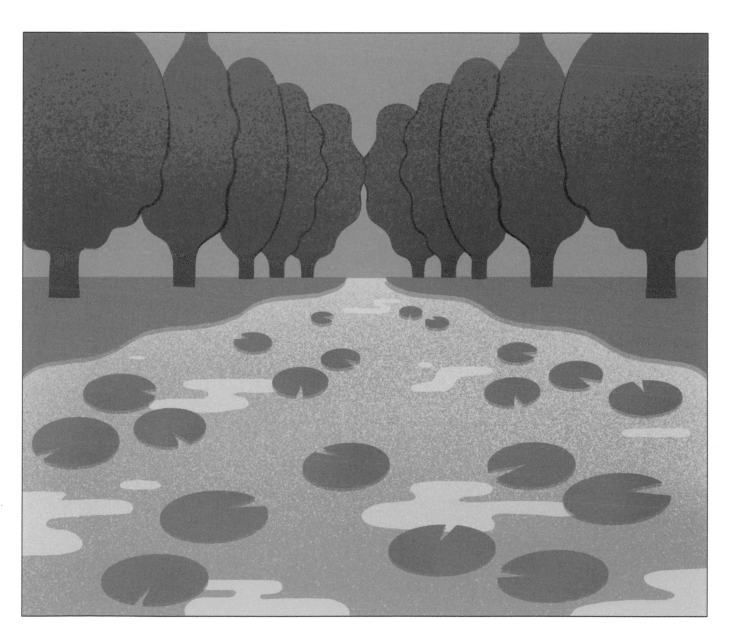

If you hadn't seen for yourself that these frogs were the same size, would you believe it? The picture's perspective creates an amazing optical illusion, making the frog toward the top of the stream look smaller.

The key to why this happens is something called the vanishing point.

First, an artist draws a horizon line across their picture, somewhere toward its top edge.

Then they mark the vanishing point somewhere along this line, usually toward the middle.

construction lines

The closer something in a painting is to this vanishing point, the smaller it needs to be. This makes it look farther away. The artist can draw a grid of construction lines to show them how big and close together things should be at different places in the picture.

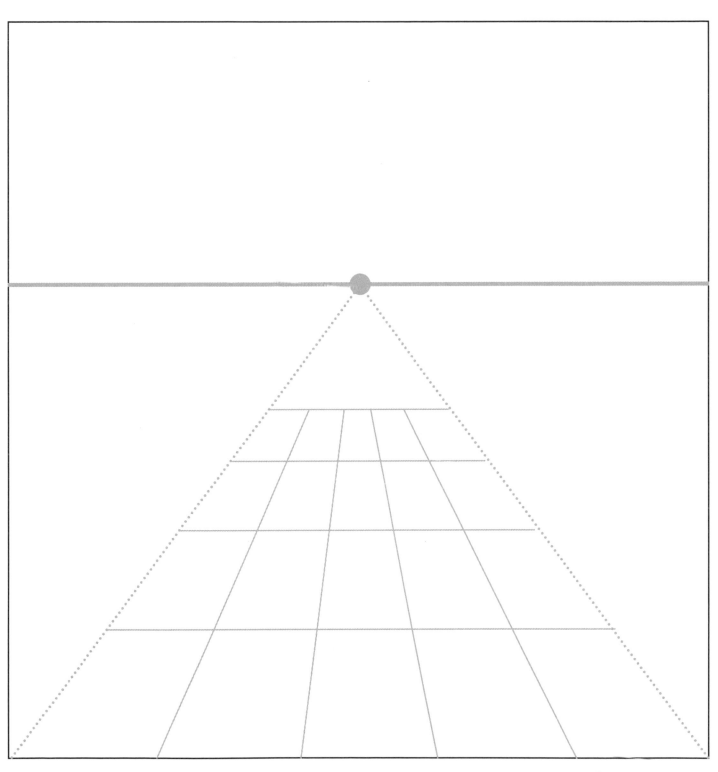

Find a natural view to draw or paint, maybe in a garden or nearby park. Notice how the trees and plants farther away look smaller? Use this perspective grid to keep the view 3-D in your painting.

SCULPTING PEOPLE

This marble statue shows Hiawatha, a popular Native American character from a long poem. Edmonia Lewis, who sculpted him while working in Italy, was of African American and Native American (Anishinaabe/Ojibwe) heritage.

Can you see how some parts of Hiawatha's face are lighter and some are darker? Where parts stand out—like the tops of his cheeks—they catch the light. Where they dip in—like the area under his nose—they are in shadow.

Edmonia Lewis
Hiawatha
1868

Try creating a 3-D drawing of a person's head and shoulders by shading in parts that would be in shadow. Look at your own face in the mirror to help! You can use crosshatching (lots of little lines that crisscross over each other) for your shading.

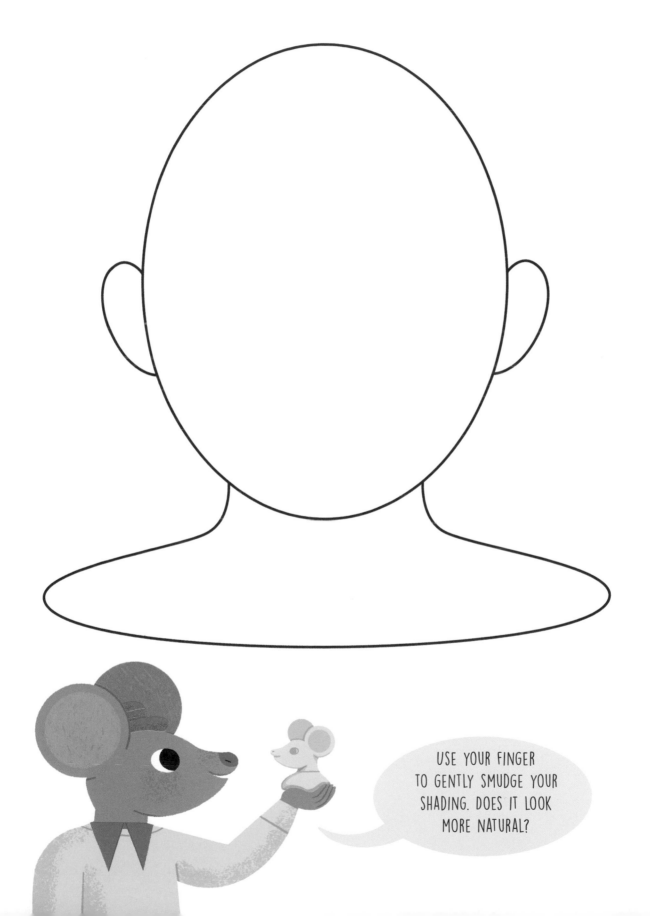

USE YOUR FINGER TO GENTLY SMUDGE YOUR SHADING. DOES IT LOOK MORE NATURAL?

Now you can carve a soap sculpture based on your 3-D drawing! Draw a head and shoulders outline on a bar of soap (the soft, creamy kind).

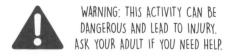

Then, ask your adult to cut it out.

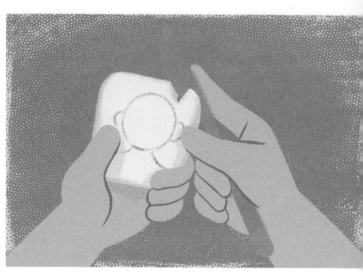

2 Use round-ended scissors, a paper clip, or a spoon to carve your sculpture. Carve most deeply in the areas where your drawing has the darkest shading.

Carving takes a bit of practice, so don't expect it to look perfect the first time! You can also leave the bar whole and focus on the facial features.

3 Try scratching in thin lines to show hair, eyebrows, and eyelashes.

 4 Finish by carefully rubbing your fingers over your sculpture. This will remove any leftover shavings and smooth its surface.

Be careful not to rub any details away!

TRY CARVING ANIMAL FACES. YOU COULD GIVE SOMEONE A SOAP PORTRAIT OF THEIR PET!

SKETCHBOOK PAGES TO FILL!

Project Editor Rosie Peet
US Senior Editor Jennette ElNaggar
Editor Vicky Armstrong
Project Art Editor Stefan Georgiou
Designer Zoë Tucker
Picture Researchers Martin Copeland,
Sumedha Chopra, and Sumita Khatwani
Production Editor Siu Yin Chan
Senior Production Controller Louise Minihane
Senior Commissioning Editor Katy Flint
Managing Art Editor Vicky Short
Publishing Director Mark Searle

First American edition published, 2023
Published in the United States by DK Publishing,
1745 Broadway, 20th Floor, New York, NY 10019

Page design copyright © 2023 Dorling Kindersley Limited
DK, a Division of Penguin Random House LLC

Text copyright © Alice Harman, 2023
Illustrations copyright © Kimberlie Clinthorne-Wong, 2023

23 24 25 26 27 10 9 8 7 6 5 4 3 2 1
001–333261–December/2023

**The Metropolitan
Museum of Art**
New York

© The Metropolitan Museum of Art

A catalog record for this book
is available from the Library of Congress.

ISBN 978-0-7440-6524-4

DK books are available at special discounts when purchased in bulk for sales promotions, premiums, fund-raising, or educational use. For details, contact: DK Publishing Special Markets, 1745 Broadway, 20th Floor, New York, NY 10019
SpecialSales@dk.com

Printed and bound in China

Acknowledgments
DK would like to thank Laura Barth, Emily Blumenthal, Leanne Graeff, Jennifer Kelaher, Stephen Mannello, Morgan Pearce, Lisa Silverman Meyers, Josh Romm, and all the curators at The Met, and Sarah Harland for proofreading.

www.dk.com
www.metmuseum.org

Picture credits
The publisher would like to thank The Metropolitan Museum of Art for their kind permission to reproduce works of art from their collection.

p. 8 Two Men Walking (c. 1939-43) by Bill Traylor. American. 1992.47; **p. 12** Textile with Animals, Birds, and Flowers (late 12th-14th century). Asian. 1988.296; **p. 14** Armor of Infante Luis, Prince of Asturias (1707-1724) (1712). Signature probably refers to Jean Drouart. French. 1989.3; **p. 18** Circus Sideshow (Parade de cirque) (1887-88) by Georges Seurat. French. 61.101.17; **p. 22** A Bouquet of Flowers (ca. 1612) by Clara Peeters. Flemish. 2020.22; **p. 24** Still Life with Apples and Pears (c. 1891-92) by Paul Cézanne. French. 61.101.3; **p. 25** The Musician's Table (1914) by Juan Gris. Spanish. 2018.216; **p. 26** Figure: Seated Couple (18th-early 19th century) by Dogon artist. Malian. 1977.394.15; **p. 28** Calligraphic Galleon (AH 1180/1766-67 CE) by 'Abd al-Qadir Hisari. Turkish. 2003.241; **p. 32** Frog Pendant (11th-16th century). Costa Rican. 1991.419.1; **p. 34** Self-Portrait (ca. 1937-38) by Leonora Carrington. Mexican. 2002.456.1 © Estate of Leonora Carrington / ARS, NY and DACS, London 202; **p. 38** Terracotta lekythos (oil flask) (ca. 550-530 BCE). Attributed to the Amasis Painter. Greek. 31.11.10; **p. 42** Interior Hanging (19th century). Sierra Leone. 1873.30; **p. 46** Garden Gathering (1640-50). Iranian. 03.9c; **p. 50** Teapot (ca. 1897-1900) by George O. Ohr. American. 2017.357.13a,b; **p. 52** Panel with striding lion (ca. 604-562 BCE). Babylonian. 31.13.1; **p. 54** Street Story Quilt (1985) by Faith Ringgold. American. 1990,237a-c © Faith Ringgold / ARS, NY and DACS, London, Courtesy ACA Galleries, New York 2023; **p. 58** Model sporting boat (ca. 1981-1875 BC). Egyptian. 20.3.6; **p. 62** Under the Wave off Kanagawa (Kanagawa oki nami ura), also known as The Great Wave, from the series Thirty-six Views of Mount Fuji (Fugaku sanjūrokkei) (ca. 1830-32) by Katsushika Hokusai. Japanese. JP1847; **p. 66** Mosaic with a Peacock and Flowers (3rd-4th century). Roman or Byzantine. 26.68; **p. 70** Bridge over a Pond of Water Lilies (1899) by Claude Monet. French. 29.100.113; **p. 74** Hiawatha (1868) by Edmonia Lewis. American. 2015.287.1